BIG ENGLISH

T0346040

Contents

Welcome to Class!

1 Look, read and match.

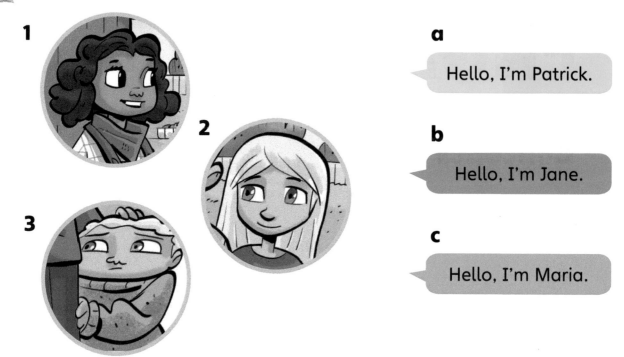

1

2

3

a

Hello, I'm Patrick.

b

Hello, I'm Jane.

c

Hello, I'm Maria.

2 Draw and write.

What's your name?

Hello, I'm _____.

3 **Look and circle.**

1 triangle / circle

2 square / circle

3 star / square

4 rectangle / triangle

5 star / rectangle

6 star / heart

4 **Read and draw.**

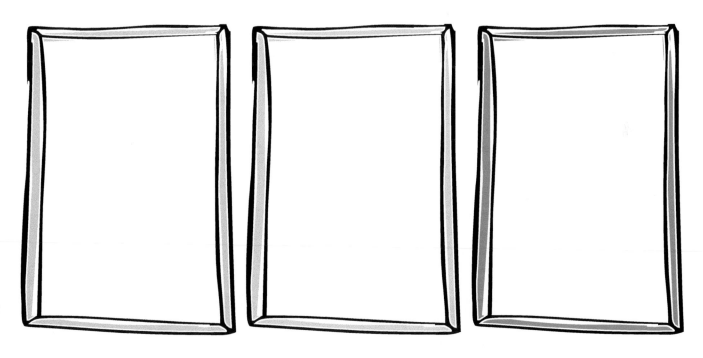

1 It's a triangle.

2 It's a star.

3 It's a heart.

5 **Read and colour.**

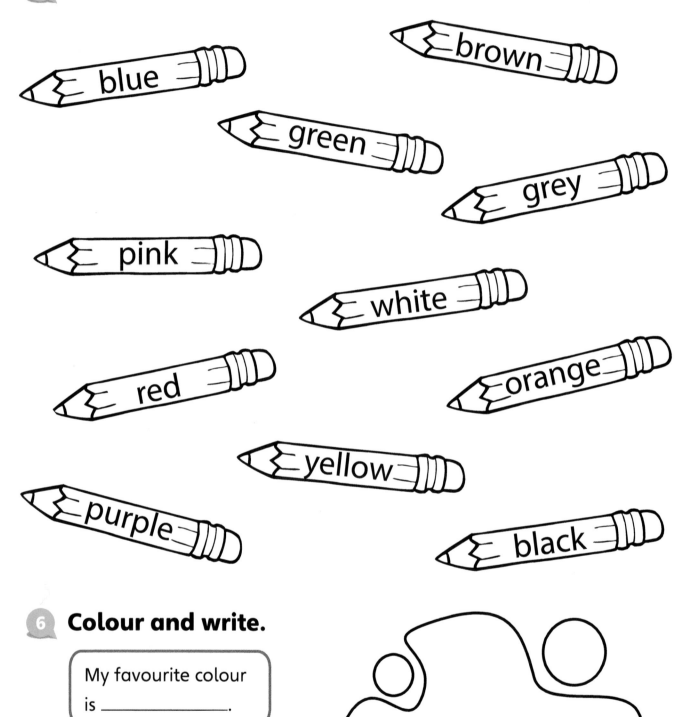

blue

brown

green

grey

pink

white

red

orange

yellow

purple

black

6 **Colour and write.**

My favourite colour
is _____.

7 Read and match.

one
two
three
four
five
six
seven
eight

nine
ten
eleven
twelve
thirteen
fourteen
fifteen

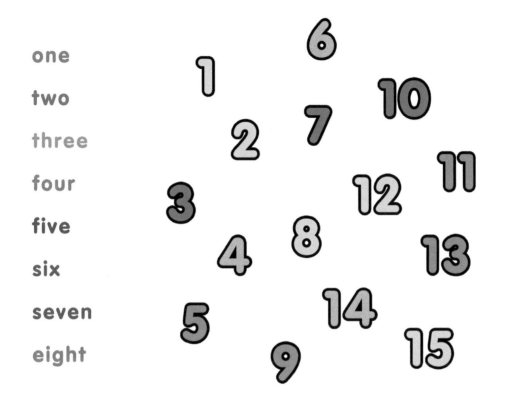

8 Join the dots. Write.

It's a _____.

9 Draw and write. How old are you?

I'm _____.

Good Morning, Class!

1 **Match, colour and say.**

1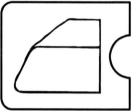

a
book

2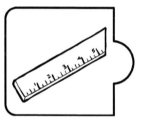

b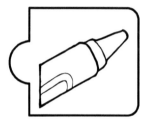
crayon

3

c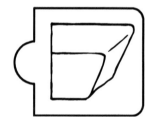
rubber

4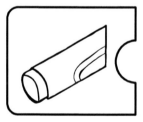

d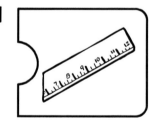
ruler

2 **Look and circle.**

1 What is it?

It's a **pen** / **marker pen**.

2 What is it?

It's a **backpack** / **desk**.

3 **Listen and sing. Then draw.**

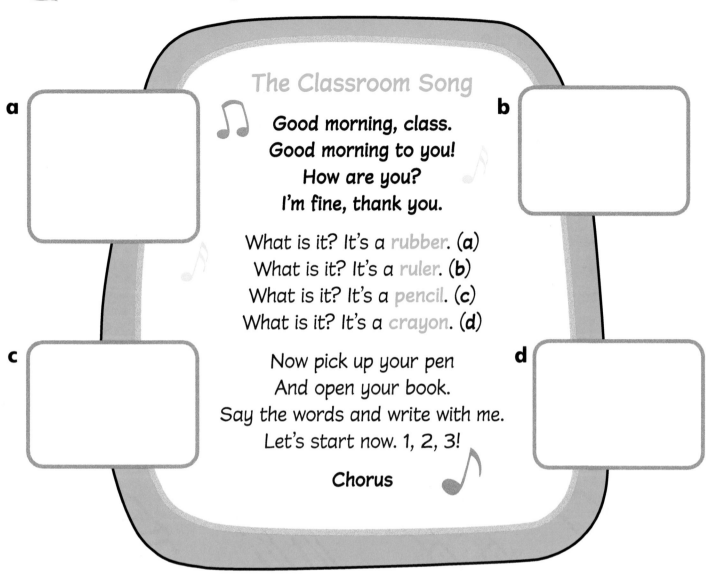

a

b

c

d

The Classroom Song

Good morning, class.
Good morning to you!
How are you?
I'm fine, thank you.

What is it? It's a rubber. (**a**)
What is it? It's a ruler. (**b**)
What is it? It's a pencil. (**c**)
What is it? It's a crayon. (**d**)

Now pick up your pen
And open your book.
Say the words and write with me.
Let's start now. 1, 2, 3!

Chorus

4 **Draw your backpack. Then write.**

This is my _____.

It's _____.

5 **Read and circle.**

Classroom Colours

What is it?

It's **a pen / a rubber**.

What are they?

They're **pencils / marker pens**.

6 **Listen and colour.**
25

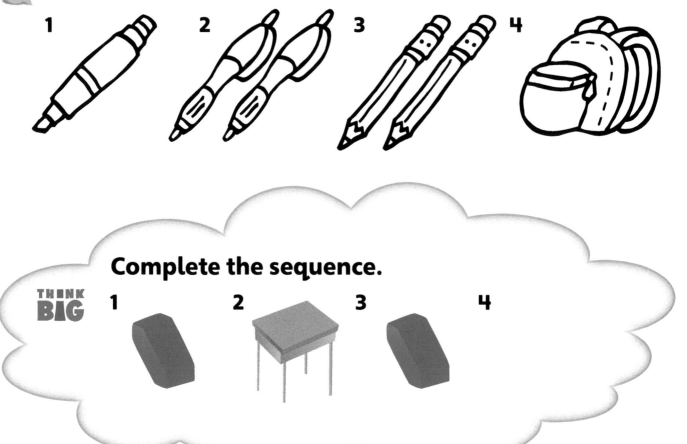

1   2   3   4

Complete the sequence.

THINK BIG

1   2   3   4

7 **Listen and ✓.**

1 **a**  ☐   **b**  ☐

2 **a**  ☐   **b**  ☐

3 **a**  ☐   **b**  ☐

4 **a**  ☐   **b**  ☐

8 **Read, draw and colour.**

1 It's a pencil.   **2** It's a book.   **3** It's a crayon.
   It's green.   It's blue.   It's yellow.

What are they?

They're...

q Match and say.

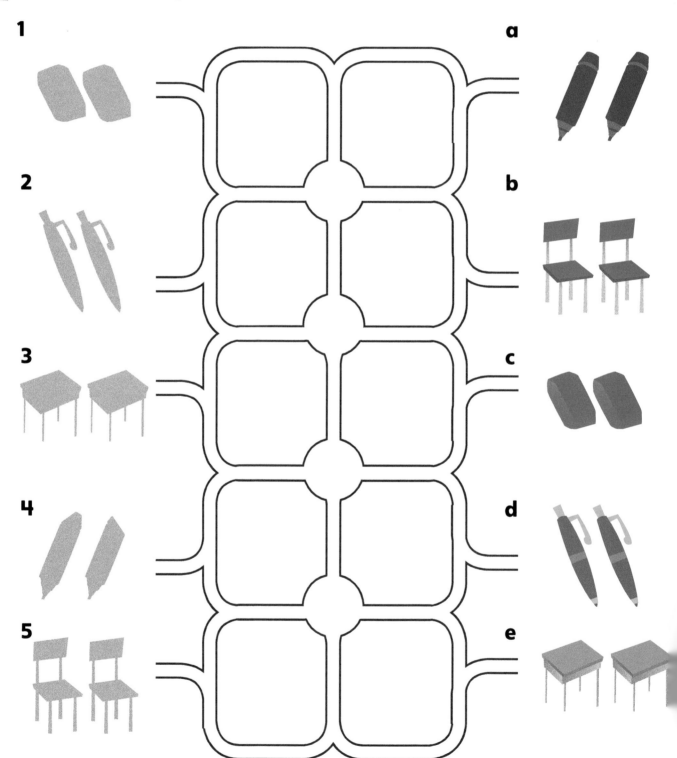

10 **Look at the pictures. Then listen, read and circle.**

1 It's a **pencil case / pencil sharpener**. It's blue, red, pink, yellow and green.

2 It's a **notebook / tablet**. It's black and white.

3 It's a **pencil / pencil sharpener**. It's red.

4 It's a **tablet / notebook**. It's green.

11 **Count and write.**

1

2

3

4

_____ rubbers   _____ marker pens   _____ rulers   _____ desk

THINK BIG **I've got 3 green pens and 1 red pen. How many pens have I got?**
I've got _____ pens.

12 Connect numbers 1 to 10. Count and write.

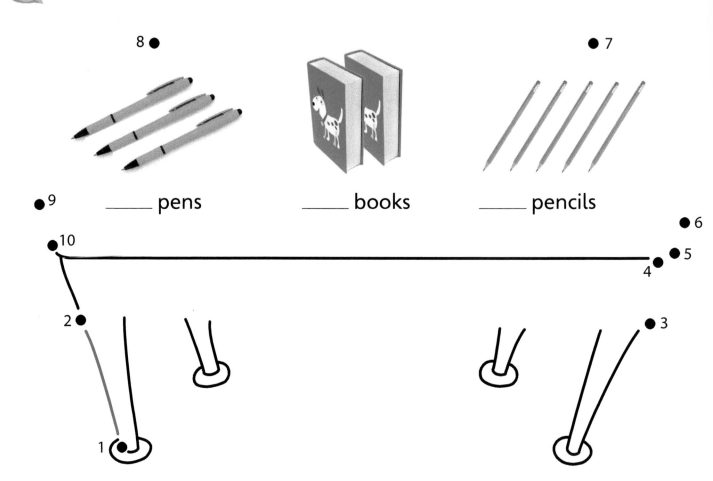

8 ●

● 7

● 9

_____ pens   _____ books   _____ pencils

● 6

● 10   ● 5

4

2 ●   ● 3

1

13 Look at 12. Read and circle T for true and F for false.

1 I've got four green pens.   **T   F**

2 I've got two books.   **T   F**

3 My pencils are red.   **T   F**

14 Look and write.

| pencils   sharpener   three |

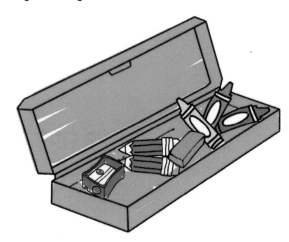

1 I've got two _____.

2 My pencil _____ is red.

3 I've got _____ crayons.

15 **Look and write.**

Don't eat!　　Don't talk!　　Look!　　Sit down!

1 _____

2 _____

3 _____

4 _____

16 **Read and circle.**

1 **Stand** / **Sit** down.

2 Don't **stand** / **sit** up!

3 **Write** / **Close** your books.

4 Don't **say** / **eat** in class!

5 **Open** / **Write** your name.

6 **Say** / **Talk** the alphabet.

17 **Look and circle.**

1
2
3

1 **Africa / China**
2 **The United States of America / Africa**
3 **China / Africa**

35
18 **Listen, read and write.**

black   grey   rulers   tablet

1 Hello! I'm Jabu. I'm seven. In Africa, my classroom is small. I've got a small desk, too. My backpack is _____.

2 Hi! I'm Katie. I'm six. In the U.S.A., I've got a big classroom. My desk is big and white. My favourite colour is white. I've got a _____, too.

3 Hello! My name is Li. I'm from China. In my classroom, I've got many books, pencils, crayons and _____. I've got a small _____ tablet.

19 **Look at 18. Read and circle T for true and F for false.**

1 Jabu has got a small classroom.   T   F
2 Katie is seven.   T   F
3 Li is from China.   T   F
4 Katie has got a brown desk.   T   F
5 Jabu has got a black backpack.   T   F
6 Li has got a big tablet.   T   F

20 **What have you got? Circle for you.**

crayons   a pink rubber

a pink backpack

a small desk

a blue pen

a big classroom

a small classroom

a notebook   a big desk

a black pen   a red pen

a blue backpack

marker pens

a white rubber   a tablet

THINK
BIG **Look at 20. Draw your things.**

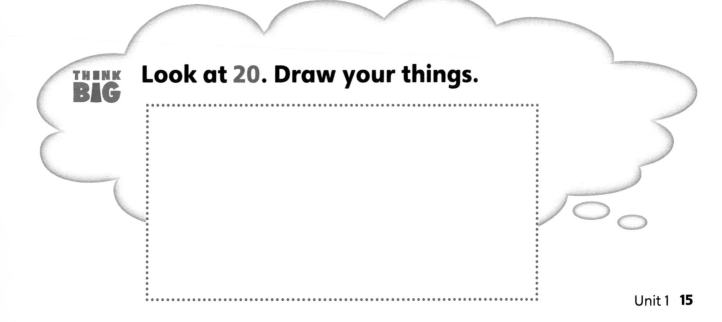

21 Read and write.

Please   you   welcome

1

Thank you.

You're _____.

2

_____ sit down.

Thank _____.

22 Draw.

I'm polite at school.

23 **Find and circle the letters a, t, p and n.**

24 **Read and circle the letters a, t, p and n.**

1 and   **2** ten   **3** pen   **4** nip

25 **Match the words with the same sounds.**

1 nap   **a** pen
2 pan   **b** and
3 ant   **c** nip

41
26 **Listen and chant.**

Pat the ant

Has got a tan.

Pat the ant

Takes a nap.

Review

27 **Read, draw and colour.**

(empty box)
---

1 I've got a pencil. It's yellow.

(empty box)
---

2 I've got a desk. It's blue.

(empty box)
---

3 I've got three marker pens. They're red.

(empty box)
---

4 I've got two books. They're green.

28 **Read and circle.**

1 What is it?
It's / They're a tablet.

2 What are they?
It's / They're notebooks.

3 What is it? It's a
pencil case / pencil sharpener.

4 What **is it / are they**?
They're pencil sharpeners.

29 **Read and match.**

1 Don't run	**a** your homework.
2 Listen	**b** on the desk.
3 Don't write	**c** to the teacher.
4 Do	**d** in class.

30 **Colour.**

1 = **red**   2 = **blue**   3 = **green**   4 = **yellow**

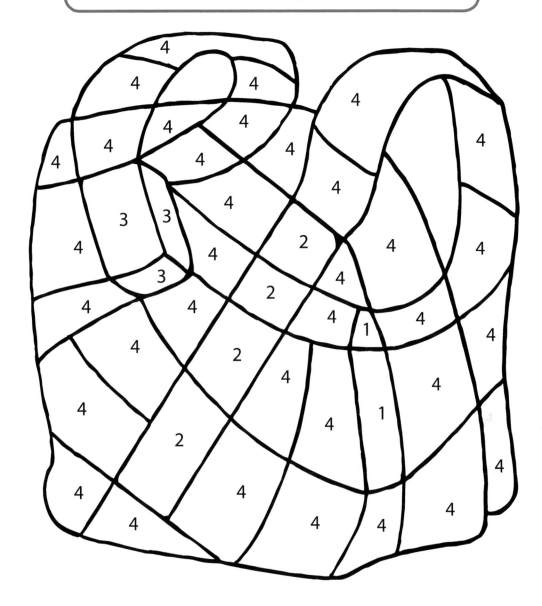

31 **Look at 30. Match.**

1 What is it? It's red.

2 What is it? It's blue.

3 What is it? It's green.

4 What is it? It's yellow.

a It's a rubber.

b It's a backpack.

c It's a crayon.

d It's a ruler.

My Family

1 **Read and match.**

grandma

grandad

sister

My family.

brother

dad

mum

2 Listen and circle. Then sing.

My Family

My family, my family!
This is my family.
He's my brother / sister
And she's my brother / sister.

My dad / mum, my dad / mum!
My sister, my brother!
We have so much fun!
I love them!

My family, my family.
I love my family!
I love them and they love me.
I love my family!

3 Draw your mum and dad. Then write.

My _____

My _____

4 **Read and point. Then read and circle.**

A Big Family

Who are they?

They're my parents.

Who's she?

She's my sister.

Oh, she's Jane.

And who's he?

He's my brother!

How many brothers and sisters have I got?

I've got...

a one brother and two sisters.

b one brother and one sister.

c two brothers and one sister.

Look at 4. Tick (✓) Tim's family.

THINK BIG

1 ☐   2 ☐

52
5 Listen and write the number.

6 **Read. Count and colour.**

7 **Look, read and match.**

1    2    3    4

a boy   **b** man   **c** woman   **d** girl

56

8 **Look at the picture. Then listen, read and circle.**

This is my family.

I'm a ¹**boy** / **girl.** My name's Ian.

This ²**man** / **boy** is my dad. This ³**girl** / **woman** is my mum.

This ⁴**boy** / **baby** is my brother. This ⁵**girl** / **boy** is my sister.

This ⁶**girl** / **woman** is my grandma and this is my grandad.

THINK BIG

Are you a boy or a girl?

I'm a _____.

9 Look, read and match.

1 This woman is my grandma.

a

b

2 This girl is my sister.

3 This woman is my mum.

c

d

4 This man is my grandad.

5 This boy is my brother.

e

10 Look and write.

| boy   girl (x2)   man (x2)   woman (x2) |

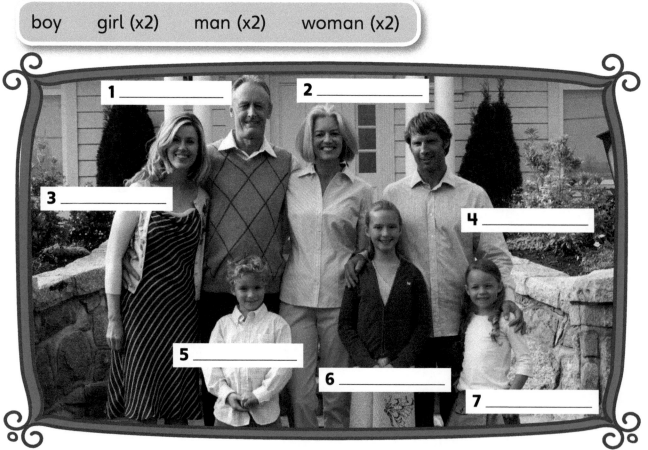

1 _____

2 _____

3 _____

4 _____

5 _____

6 _____

7 _____

58

11 Listen and ✓.

1

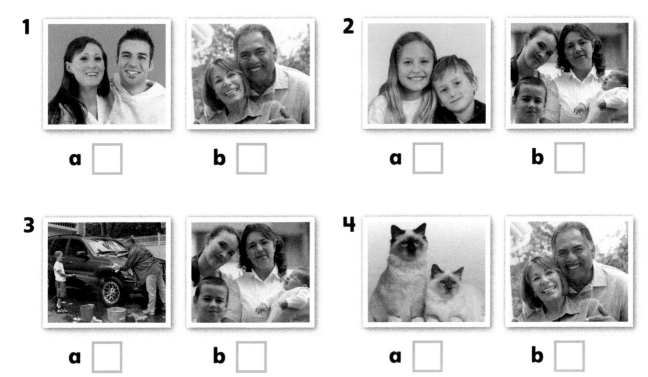

a ☐   b ☐

2

a ☐   b ☐

3

a ☐   b ☐

4

a ☐   b ☐

12 Read and circle.

1 This is my **brother** / **sisters**.

2 These are my **grandma** / **brothers**.

3 This is my **grandparents** / **grandad**.

4 These are my **parents** / **baby brother**.

13 Look, read and match.

a

1 His name's Dan.

b

2 Her name's Amy.

14 **Look and write. Who are they?**

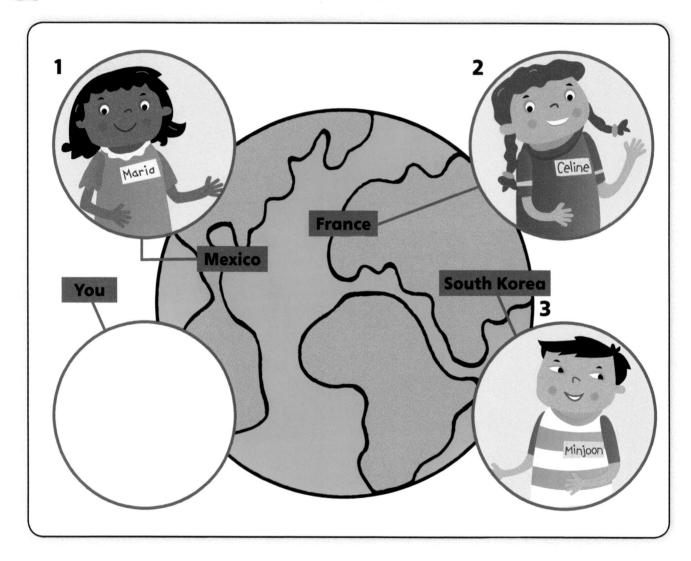

1 Her name's _____. She's from Mexico.

2 Her name's _____. She's from France.

3 His name's _____. He's from South Korea.

15 **Look at 14 and draw. What's your name? Where are you from?**

My name's _____. I'm from _____.

16 **Listen, read and circle.**

This is my family and these are my friends. Maria is a ¹**girl** / **friend**. She's my ²**sister** / **best friend**. Minjoon is a ³**family** / **boy**. He's my friend, too. This is my ⁴**sister** / **friend**. Her name's Celine. I love my ⁵**family** / **sister** and friends!

17 **Look at 16. Read and circle T for true and F for false.**

1 Maria is a boy.	**T**	**F**
2 Minjoon is a girl.	**T**	**F**
3 Maria is my best friend.	**T**	**F**
4 Celine is my brother.	**T**	**F**
5 I love my family and friends.	**T**	**F**

18 **Find and write the words.**

1 _____ steb ndeirf

2 _____ dsreinf

3 _____ ylmaif

Draw your best friend's family.

THINK BIG

63

19 **Listen and match.**

1

Can I help you?

Yes, thank you.

a Tommy helps his mum.   **b** Pam helps her brother.

2

Please help me.

OK. I can help you.

20 **Draw.**

I can help!

21 **Find and circle the letters i, s, b and d.**

22 **Read and circle the letters i, s, b and d.**

1 dad   **2** in   **3** bat   **4** sit

23 **Match the words with the same sounds.**

1 dad   **a** sad
2 in   **b** dip
3 sit   **c** it

24 68 **Listen and chant.**

Don't sit, sit, sit
On a pin, pin, pin
It's bad, bad, bad
To sit on a pin!

25 Find the family words. Colour them green.

My Family

name

help

mum

parents

one

no

grandad

dad

yes

grandma

sister

please

thank you

grandparents

two

baby brother

colour

and

 26 Read and match.

	my parents.
This is	my family.
These are	my friends.
	my best friend.

Look and match. Then read.

1   **a** man

2   **b** girl

3   **c** boy

4   **d** woman

28 Draw your family. Then say.

This is my family.

My Body

1 **Read and match.**

eye   head

nose   ear

neck   mouth

leg   finger

hand   arm

toe   foot

2 **Draw your friend.**

76

3 Listen and circle. Then sing.

My Body Song

Have you got two eyes / ears?
Have you got one mouth / nose?
Have you got two eyes?
Yes, I have. Yes, I have.

I've got ten fingers / toes.
I've got ten toes.
I've got two hands / feet
And one big nose!

And have you got long hair / legs?
And have you got short hair / arms?
And have you got small hands?
I sing my body song, my body song,
I sing my body song again!

4 Read and write.

| one | ten | ten | two | two |

1 I've got _____ fingers.

2 I've got _____ nose.

3 I've got _____ toes.

4 I've got _____ ears.

5 I've got _____ eyes.

5 Read and match.

a Yes, he has! Bobo has got one eye!

b No. My teddy bear has got small ears.

Brown? Oh! Has he got one eye?

Lost Teddy

Is this your teddy bear?

_____

_____

6 Read and circle Yes or No.

1 Is Bobo green?   **Yes**   **No**

2 Has Bobo got small ears?   **Yes**   **No**

3 Has he got long legs?   **Yes**   **No**

4 Has he got one eye?   **Yes**   **No**

THINK BIG

This is _____. He's my favourite teddy bear.
He's got **big / small** eyes.
He's got **big / small** ears.
He's got **short / long** legs.

7 **Read, match and circle.**

1

Has he got long legs?

**Yes, he has. /
No, he hasn't.**

2

Has it got short ears?

**Yes, it has. /
No, it hasn't.**

3

Has she got long hair?

**Yes, she has. /
No, she hasn't.**

8 **Listen and ✓.**

1 a  □   b  □

2 a  □   b  □

9 **Connect numbers 1 to 10. What is it?**

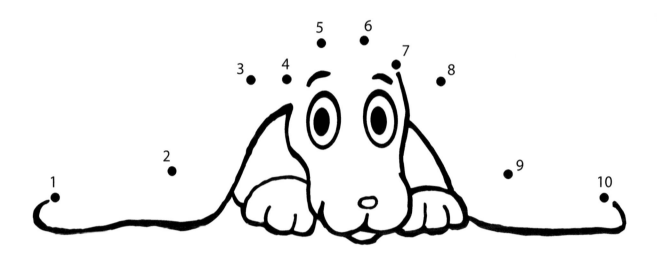

10 **Look at 9. Circle the answer.**

1 Has it got long ears? **Yes, it has. / No, it hasn't.**

2 Has it got small eyes? **Yes, it has. / No, it hasn't.**

3 Has it got a big nose? **Yes, it has. / No, it hasn't.**

11 Look and circle.

1

2

3

4

see / hear   taste / smell   see / taste   hear / smell

83
12 Listen, read and write.

a 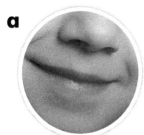   **b**    **c** 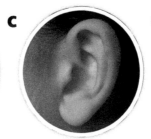   **d**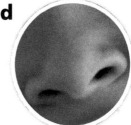

1 I hear with my ears. I hear a song. ☐

2 I see with my eyes. I see a star. ☐

3 I taste with my mouth. I taste ice cream. ☐

4 I smell with my nose. I smell flowers. ☐

THINK BIG

I see...	I smell...	I taste...	I hear...

13 Read and write.

ears	eyes	mouth	nose

1 I've got one _____. I smell a flower.

2 I've got two _____. I see a picture.

3 I've got one _____. I taste cake.

4 I've got two _____. I hear music.

14 Find and circle.

ears	eyes	hear	mouth	nose	see	smell	taste

e	a	r	s	n	n	a	q
y	z	g	m	o	u	t	h
e	n	v	e	s	l	a	e
s	e	e	l	e	c	s	a
p	b	l	l	k	d	t	r
v	d	j	m	v	g	e	x

15 **Read and circle.**

1 It's a / It's an chair.

2 It's a / It's an egg.

3 It's a / They're fingers.

16 **Complete the chart. Write It's a, It's an and They're.**

It's a marker pen.	They're marker pens.
1 _____ triangle.	They're triangles.
2 _____ orange.	They're oranges.
It's an egg.	**3** _____ eggs.

17 **Look and match.**

1 It's a

2 They're

3 It's an

a toes.

b backpack.

c apple.

18 **Look and match.**

1 yellow   a

2 white   b

3 brown   c

4 purple   d

5 orange   e

6 black   f

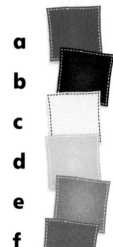

86

19 **Look at the pictures. Then listen, read and write the colours.**

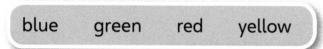

blue   green   red   yellow

1 France has got a _____, white and red flag.

2 The flag from South Africa is _____, green, yellow, blue, black and white.

3 The green, _____ and blue flag is from Brazil.

4 Ireland has got a _____, white and orange flag.

20 **Look at 19. Read and circle T for true and F for false.**

1 The flag from France is green, white and red.　　T　　F

2 Ireland has got an orange, white and green flag.　　T　　F

3 The yellow, green, red, blue, white and black flag
　is from South Africa.　　T　　F

4 Brazil has a yellow, red and green flag.　　T　　F

21 **Find and write the words.**

1 _____ lpruep

2 _____ earogn

3 _____ worbn

4 _____ ihetw

5 _____ llowye

6 _____ klacb

THINK BIG **Draw a flag for a new country! Then write the colours.**

_____

_____

_____

90

22 **Listen and match. Then sing.**

Keep Clean

1
Every day
Before I eat
And after I play,
I wash my hands.

2
With a lot of soap
It's easy, you see.
Rinse with water
Just like me.

3
Dry them well and
Sing this song.
Keep your hands clean
All day long!

a

b

c

23 **Draw.**

I keep clean.

24 **Find and circle the letters e, c, g and m.**

25 **Read and circle the letters e, c, g and m.**

1 gas   **2** map   **3** cap   **4** pen

26 **Match the words with the same sounds.**

1 get   **a** cat
2 mat   **b** map
3 cap   **c** gas

95
27 **Listen and chant.**

The cap is on the cat.

The cat goes on the map.

The pen goes on the bed.

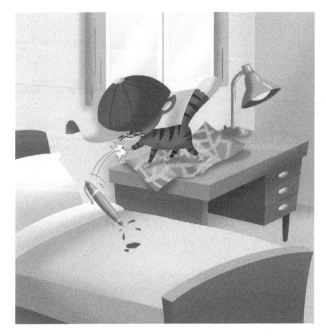

Review

28 **Read and circle.**

1

Has he got a long nose?

Yes, he has. / No, he hasn't.

2

Has he got small feet?

Yes, he has. / No, he hasn't.

3

Has he got short hair?

Yes, he has. / No, he hasn't.

29 **Read and circle.**

1 **It's a / It's an** nose.
2 **They're / It's an** ears.
3 **It's an / It's a** eye.
4 **It's a / They're** mouth.
5 **It's an / They're** eyes.

30 **Look and write.**

arm

eye

finger

leg

mouth

nose

1 _____

2 _____

3 _____

4 _____

5 _____

6 _____

31 **Draw and match.**

This is me.

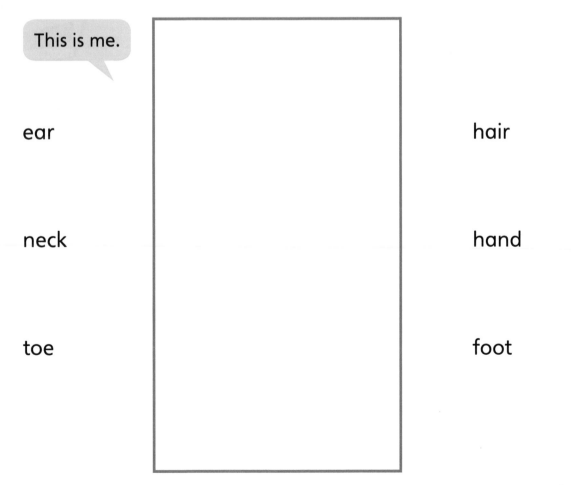

ear   hair

neck   hand

toe   foot

1 Look, find and number.

CLASS

1	crayons
2	rubbers
3	pens
4	rulers

2 Look and ✓.
Tom's got:

My List

☐ pens
☐ pencils
☐ rubbers
☐ a ruler

3 Think and draw. Tom hasn't got:

SCHOOL SUPPLIES →

BIG SALE!

FAMILY

5 dad

6 mum

7 sister

BODY

8 arm

9 eye

10 hand

My Favourite Clothes

1 **Colour. Then match.**

| a red blouse | blue trousers | a yellow jacket |

1 = **red**

2 = **blue**

3 = **yellow**

| yellow boots | a blue skirt | red shoes | red gloves |

2 **Draw.**

My Favourite Clothes

3 **Listen and circle. Then chant.**

What Are You Wearing?

What are you wearing?
I'm wearing a T-shirt / shirt.
What are you wearing?
I'm wearing a skirt / blouse.

What's he wearing?
He's wearing new trousers / shorts.
What's he wearing?
He's wearing old shoes / boots.

What's she wearing?
She's wearing a red / blue hat.
What's she wearing?
She's wearing black / pink shoes.

4 Match. Then read and colour.

1

My Favourite Hat!

I'm wearing a green hat. It's my favourite hat!

2

What's Tim wearing?

He's wearing a brown hat. It's his favourite hat.

3

What's Maria wearing?

She's wearing a purple hat. It's her favourite hat.

a

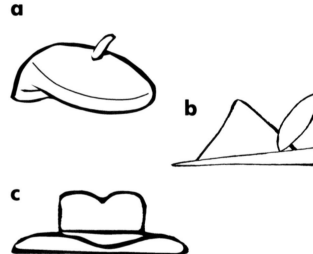

b

c

Which clothes are the same? Circle.

THINK BIG

5 Listen and ✓.

1 a   b

2 a   b

3 a   b

4 a   b

6 Look. Read and circle.

I'm wearing **boots** / **shoes**, a hat and a **green** / **yellow** jacket.

1

I'm wearing a **green** / **yellow** T-shirt, trousers and blue **boots** / **shoes**.

2

7 **Colour and write.**

b = **brown**	g = **green**	o = **orange**
p = **purple**	r = **red**	y = **yellow**

1 He's wearing an orange _____.

2 He's wearing a yellow _____.

3 He's wearing purple _____.

4 He's wearing brown _____.

5 He's wearing green _____.

gloves

hat

shirt

shoes

trousers

8 **Look and ✓.**

cold hot	hot dry	dry wet	wet cold
☐ ☐	☐ ☐	☐ ☐	☐ ☐

9 **Find and write. Then listen and circle.** 114

desert   jungle   mountains

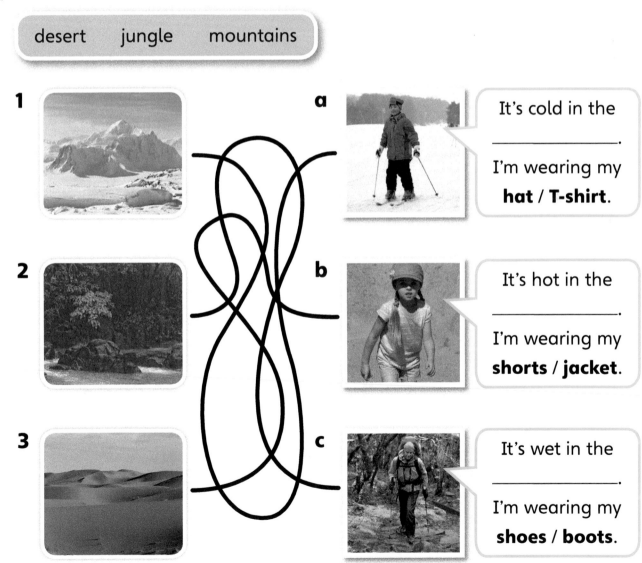

a
It's cold in the
_____.
I'm wearing my
hat / T-shirt.

b
It's hot in the
_____.
I'm wearing my
shorts / jacket.

c
It's wet in the
_____.
I'm wearing my
shoes / boots.

10 Look at 9. Read and circle **T** for true and **F** for false.

1 It's hot. I'm wearing my boots.   T   F

2 It's wet. I'm wearing my jacket.   T   F

3 It's cold. I'm wearing my shorts.   T   F

4 It's hot. I'm wearing my hat.   T   F

11 Look and write. Then colour.

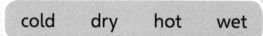

cold   dry   hot   wet

1 _____

2 _____

3 _____

4 _____

It's wet. What's she wearing? Circle.

THINK
BIG   jacket   trousers

dress

shorts   blouse

shirt

boots   shoes

hat   skirt

socks

gloves

12 **Look at the pictures. Then listen and ✓.**

1 She's seven. ☐   **2** He's six. ☐   **3** They're five. ☐

She's nine. ☐   He's ten. ☐   They're eight. ☐

13 **Put the words in order. Draw lines.**

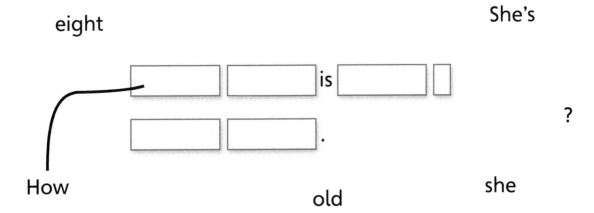

eight

She's

How

old

she

?

is

14 **Read and write.**

old   six   ten   two

My name's Mark. I'm six. Ann is my sister.
She's young. She's ¹_____. Leo is my
brother. He's old. He's ²_____. I've
got two best friends. They're ³_____,
too! Mr. Williams is my teacher. He's very ⁴_____!

15 Look and match.

1 I've got a black and white hat.

2 I've got a pink and purple woolly hat.

3 I've got a blue cap.

a

b

c

119 16 Listen and read. Then draw and colour.

Here are some very funny hats! Let's look at them.

1 This hat is small. It's a girl's hat. It's yellow. It's got a dog on it.

2 This hat is very funny! It's big and blue. It's got red pencils on it.

3 This hat is green. It's got shoes on it! It's got a pink shoe and a purple shoe on it.

17 **Look at 16. Read and ✓ or ✗.**

1 The small hat is yellow. _____

2 The big hat has got a dog on it. _____

3 The red pencils are on the blue hat. _____

4 The shoes are on the green hat. _____

18 **Read and write. Then find and write the word.**

1 Some hats have got on them.

2 Some hats have got many .

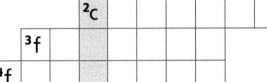

3 Some hats have got big on them.

4 Some hats have got long on them.

People look at the funny hats at A _ _ _ _.

THINK BIG **Draw a party hat!**

19 **Look, read and write.**

dress   trousers   white

They're wearing traditional clothes from the Philippines. He's wearing a _____ shirt and _____. She's wearing a white _____.

20 **Draw.**

I'm wearing traditional clothes.

21 **Find and circle the letters o, k and ck.**

22 **Read and circle the letters o, k and ck.**

1 on   **2** kid   **3** sock   **4** dog

23 **Match the words with the same sounds.**

1 pot   **a** pick
2 neck   **b** kit
3 kid   **c** dog

24 **Listen and chant.**

125

Put on your socks,
Put on your kit.
Kick the ball,
Kick, kick, kick!

25 Look and write.

| blouse | boots | dress | gloves | hat | jacket | shirt |
| shoes | shorts | skirt | socks | trousers | T-shirt |

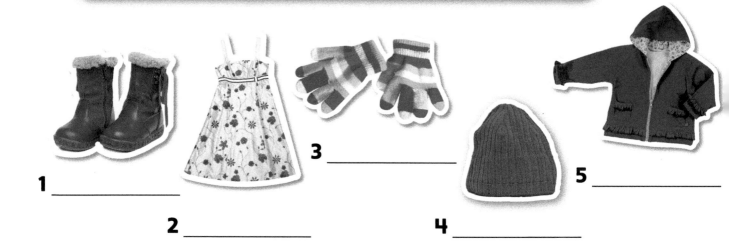

1 _____

2 _____

3 _____

4 _____

5 _____

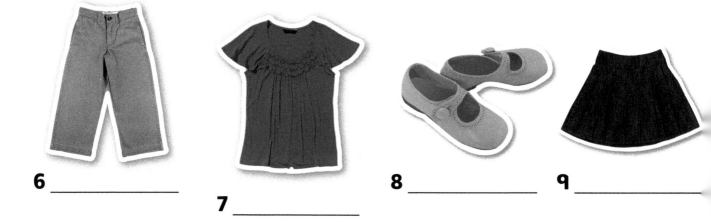

6 _____

7 _____

8 _____

9 _____

10 _____

11 _____

12 _____

13 _____

26 **Look and colour. Then listen and ✓.**

1 = **green**	2 = yellow	3 = **black**
4 = blue	5 = orange	6 = **purple**

1 a   b   **2** a   b

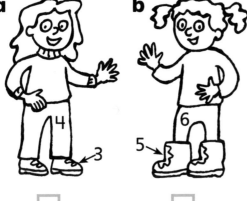  

☐   ☐   ☐   ☐

3 a   b   **4** a   b

☐   ☐   ☐   ☐

 27 **Read, circle and match.**

1 How old **is** / **are** they?   **a** I'm eight.

2 How old **is** / **are** he?   **b** They're seven.

3 How old **is** / **are** you?   **c** She's ten.

4 How old **is** / **are** she?   **d** He's three.

Busy at Home

1 **Read and match.**

1 She's getting dressed. ☐

2 She's drinking and he's reading. ☐

3 He's having a bath. ☐

4 He's making lunch. ☐

5 He's eating. ☐

2 Listen and write. Then sing.

breakfast   face   hair   lunch   phone   teeth

What Are You Doing?

I'm brushing my ¹_____.
I'm combing my ²_____.
   I'm busy. I'm busy.
   What are you doing?

I'm eating my ³_____.
I'm washing my ⁴_____.
   I'm busy. I'm busy.
   What are you doing?

I'm talking on the ⁵_____.
I'm making my ⁶_____.
   I'm busy. I'm busy.
   What are you doing?

Chorus

3 Draw.

He's sleeping.	She's playing.

Story

4 Read and write.

1 What are they doing?
They're _____.

2 What is Patrick doing?
He's _____.

3 What's she doing?
She's _____.

THINK BIG

What are you and your friend doing?

We're _____.

5 Listen and number.

6 Circle.

1  **He's / She's** sleeping.

2  **He's / She's** talking on the phone.

3  **He's / She's** drinking.

7 **Write I'm, He's or She's.**

1 What's she doing? _____ washing.

2 What are you doing? _____ having a bath.

3 What's he doing? _____ combing his hair.

8 **Look and match.**

1 What are you doing, Dad? **a** I'm drawing.

2 What are you doing, Anna? **b** I'm reading.

3 What are you doing, Mum? **c** I'm eating.

4 What are you doing, Grandad? **d** I'm making lunch.

9 **Draw. What are you doing?**

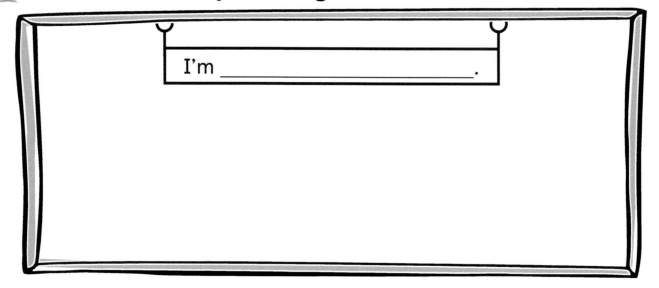

I'm _____.

10 **Read and write.**

flat   houseboat   lighthouse   yurt

1 _____ **2** _____ **3** _____ **4** _____

11 **Look and listen. Then read and circle.**

1 My home is a **lighthouse / flat**. It's very tall. It's got **six / seven** windows. They're **circles / squares**. It's got one big door. It's a square.

2 This is my home. It's a **yurt / houseboat**. It's very small. It's got **four / five** windows. They're **triangles / circles**. The door is a rectangle.

THINK BIG Find and draw three things in your house that are a square, a circle and a rectangle.

12 **Look, read and ✓ or ✗.**

1 It's got four small windows. ☐

2 The windows are rectangles. ☐

3 It's a flat. ☐

4 It's got big windows. ☐

5 The table is a triangle. ☐

6 It's a houseboat. ☐

13 **Read and draw.**

This is my home.
It's a lighthouse.

It's green and white.
It's very tall.

It's got six big windows.
They're circles.

It's got a square door.
It's brown.

Look, read and match.

1

2

3

a It's small.   **b** It's orange.   **c** They're grey.

 Put the words in order. Draw lines.

purple

[ ] [ ] is [ ] [ ]

It's

[ ] [ ] .

?

What

colour

it

 Read and circle. Write It's or They're.

1 What colour **is /**
are it?

_____ orange.

2 What colour is **it /**
they?

_____ green.

3 What colour **is /**
are they?

_____ pink.

17 **Look and circle.**

1 It's a **house** / **flat**.

2 It's a **flat** / **caravan**.

3 It's a **caravan** / **house**.

18 **Listen, read and write.**

144

| big | caravan | circle | rectangle | small | square |

My home is a caravan.
It's on a ¹_____ site.
It's got a ²_____ kitchen.
It's a ³_____. It's got a
living room. The living room has
got a ⁴_____ TV. It's a
⁵_____. I've got a small
bedroom. It's got a window. It's
a ⁶_____. My home is
comfortable.

19 **Look at 18. Circle T for true and F for false.**

1 My home is a flat.   T   F

2 It's got a big kitchen.   T   F

3 The living room is a rectangle.   T   F

4 The bedroom is small.   T   F

5 The bedroom window is a circle.   T   F

20 **Read and match.**

1 There are eight chairs in the   **a** bedroom.

2 Mum and Dad sleep in the   **b** kitchen.

3 The big TV is in the   **c** dining room.

4 There's a very small table in the   **d** living room.

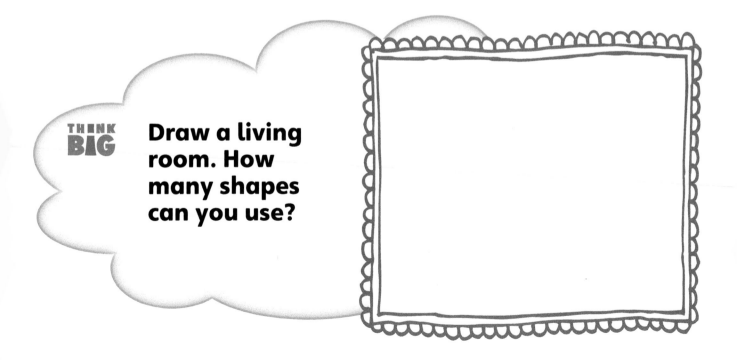

THINK BIG **Draw a living room. How many shapes can you use?**

146
21 Listen and write.

cleaning   drying   helping   washing

1 She's _____ her room.

2 She's _____ the dishes.

3 He's _____ the dishes.

4 She's _____ her parents.

22 Draw.

I'm helping at home.

23 **Find and circle the letters u, f and ff.**

24 **Read and circle the letters u, f and ff.**

1 up   **2** fan   **3** puff   **4** bus

25 **Match the words with the same sounds.**

1 sun   **a** fan
2 off   **b** up
3 fog   **c** puff

 26 **Listen and chant.**

151

> We're having fun,
> Running in the sun.
> Up, up, up!
> Puff, puff, puff!

27 **Look, read and match.**

a

b

1 I'm brushing my teeth.

c

2 I'm having a bath.

d

3 I'm making lunch.

4 I'm eating.

e

5 I'm sleeping.

f

6 I'm playing.

7 I'm combing my hair.

g

h

8 I'm drinking.

9 I'm reading.

i

10 I'm talking on the phone.

j

11 I'm washing my face.

k

12 I'm getting dressed.

l

28 Look and write.

| are | is | It's | they | They're | What |

1

Look at the book.

What colour _____ it?

_____ blue.

2

Look at the gloves.

_____ colour

_____ _____?

_____ purple.

29 Colour the shapes. What is it?

| ☐ = green |
| ◯ = **black** |
| ☐ = yellow |
| △ = **red** |

What is it?   It's a c__t.

On the Farm

1 **Look and write. Then circle.**

cow   duck   horse

1

It's a _____.
It's **eating** / **flying**.

2

It's a _____.
It's **sleeping** / **running**.

3

It's a _____.
It's **running** / **flying**.

2 Listen and match. Then chant.

a

Look at the Animals

Look over here!
Look over there!
There are animals
Everywhere!

What is it?
It's a duck.
What's it doing?
It's flying up high!

What is it?
It's a dog!
What's it doing?
It's jumping with the frogs!

What are they?
They're goats!
What are they doing?
They're eating some oats!

Chorus

b

c

d

3 Write. Then draw.

This is my favourite
farm animal. Look.
It's a _____.

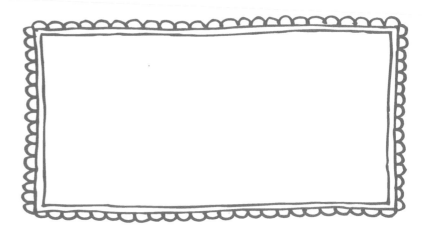

4 Read and number.

Oh, no! It's eating your skirt! ☐

It's jumping. ☐

They're running. ☐

It's flying. ☐

THINK BIG **Which sentence is wrong? Tick (✓) or cross (✗).**
The frog is jumping. ☐   The cat is flying. ☐
The horse is running. ☐

5 Listen and number.

6 Look and write.

> eating   flying   jumping   running

1 It's _____.

2 It's _____.

3 It's _____.

4 It's _____.

7 **Look and circle.**

1 It's / They're jumping.

2 It's / They're eating.

3 It's / They're flying.

4 It's / They're running.

8 **Draw.**

What's the cat doing?
It's sleeping.

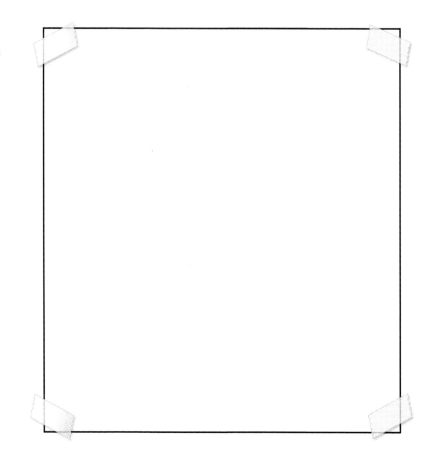

9 **Listen. Then colour, match and circle.**

1 This cow is...   **2** This chicken is...   **3** This dog is...   **4** This cat is...

a

A baby chicken is called a **calf** / **chick.**

b

A baby dog is called a **kitten** / **puppy.**

c

A baby cat is called a **calf** / **kitten.**

d

A baby cow is called a **puppy** / **calf.**

THINK BIG

Circle the picture that is wrong.

a  **b**  **c**

10 **Look and write.**

cat　　chick　　chicken　　dog　　kitten　　puppy

1

A baby

_____

is called a

_____.

2

A baby

_____

is called a

_____.

3

A baby

_____

is called a

_____.

11 **What's your favourite baby animal? Draw and write.**

My favourite baby animal is a _____.

A _____ is a baby _____.

12 Look, listen and number.

a

b

c

d

e

f

13 Complete the table.

| he | her | I | its | their | your |

1 _____	my
you	**2** _____
3 _____	his
she	**4** _____
it	**5** _____
we	our
they	**6** _____

14 **Look and circle.**

1 horse / snake

2 rabbit / hamster

3 mouse / dog

4 cat / canary

15 **Listen, read and match.**

171

a

1 I've got a pet canary. He's yellow. His name's Tom Bird.

b

2 This is my pet snake. She's green. Her name's Samantha.

c

3 I've got a pet mouse. She's small and white. Her name's Zoe.

d

4 I've got a pet hamster. He's brown. His name's Charlie.

16 **Look at 15. Read and write.**

| brown | green | yellow | white |

1 The pet hamster is _____.

2 The pet canary is _____.

3 The pet mouse is _____.

4 The pet snake is _____.

17 **Find and write the words.**

1 _____ ncayra

2 _____ mharets

3 _____ uesmo

4 _____ eknsa

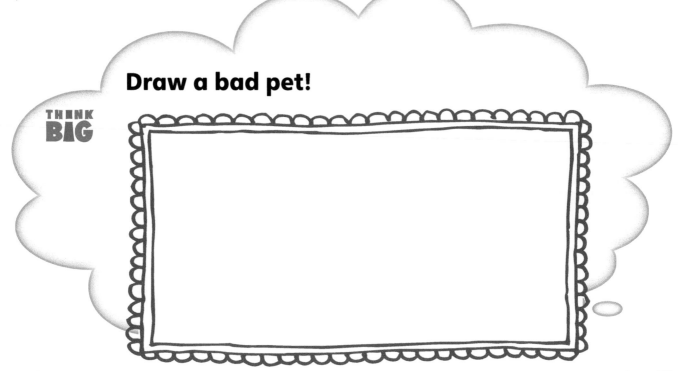

Draw a bad pet!

THINK
BIG

173
18 **Listen and write. Then match.**

brushing   feeding   playing   walking

a  ☐

b  ☐

c  ☐

d  ☐

1 I'm _____ the dog.

2 I'm _____ with the cat.

3 I'm _____ the chicks.

4 I'm _____ the horse.

19 **Draw.**

I'm playing with the cat.

20 **Find and circle the letters r, h and j.**

21 **Read and circle the letters r, h and j.**

1 rat **2** hat **3** jam **4** run

22 **Match the words with the same sounds.**

1 red   **a** hut
2 hen   **b** rock
3 jam   **c** job

23 **Listen and chant.**

A red hen in
A red hat
Is eating red jam.
Run, red hen, run!

24 Look, read and circle.

1

1 It's a **dog** / **cat**.

2 It's a **goat** / **dog**.

2

3 It's a **cow** / **sheep**.

3

4

4 It's a **frog** / **sheep**.

5 It's a **turtle** / **horse**.

5

6

6 It's a **chicken** / **horse**.

7 It's a **duck** / **chicken**.

7

8 It's a **frog** / **dog**.

8

9 It's a **cat** / **chicken**.

9

10 It's a **goat** / **cow**.

10

Look and read. Then circle and write.

| eating | flying | jumping | running | sleeping |

What are they doing?

1 What are they doing?
It's / They're

_____.

2 What's it doing?
It's / They're

_____.

3 What are they doing?
It's / They're

_____.

4 What's it doing?
It's / They're

_____.

5 What are they doing?
It's / They're

_____.

26 **Read and write.**

| Her | His | Its | my | our | your |

I've got a hamster and a cat. They're ¹_____ pets. My brother has got a snake. ²_____ snake is green and brown.

My sister has got a canary. ³_____ canary is very small. ⁴_____ feathers are yellow. There are four pets in ⁵_____ family!

Have you got a pet in ⁶_____ house?

THINK BIG

1 **Look, find and number.**

2 **Look and ✓.**
What is Sue wearing?

- [ ] a hat
- [ ] a T-shirt
- [ ] boots
- [ ] trousers
- [ ] a jacket

CLOTHES

1 dress
2 shoes
3 trousers
4 shirt

Sue

Look at 1 and draw.
What other animals can you see?

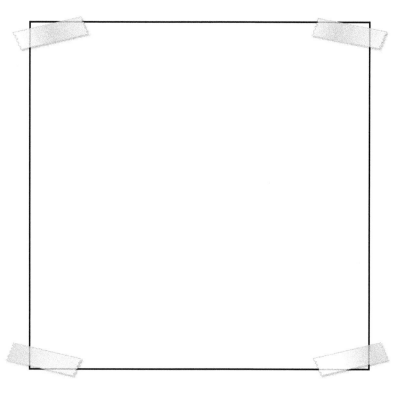

AT HOME

5 sleeping
6 talking on the phone
7 drinking

ANIMALS

8 cat
9 duck
10 turtle

unit 7 Party Time

1 Match.

1

2

milk | fruit
a | **b**
c | **d**
juice | pizza

3

4

2 Look at 1. Write.

1 She's drinking _____. **2** He's drinking _____.

3 They're eating _____. **4** She's eating _____.

Listen and number. Then sing.

a

b

c

d

It's My Party!

Welcome, friends.
Please sit down.
It's time for my party!
With games and a clown!

I've got pizza, chicken, (**1**)
Salad, too. (**2**)
Fruit, cake (**3**)
And ice cream for you! (**4**)

Or put some pasta (**5**)
On your plate.
With juice or milk (**6**)
It sure tastes great.

Thanks for the presents.
What a great day!
Let's eat and drink
And play, play, play.

e

f

Draw.

I'm eating chips and I'm drinking water.

5 **Read and write.**

1 Tim's party is on _____. **2** Tim's got _____.

3 Maria's got _____. **4** Patrick's got _____
and _____.

THINK BIG

Write the days in order.
Then circle your favourite day.

Monday _____ _____ Thursday

_____ Saturday _____

6 Look and write.

> I've got fruit.   I've got pizza.

What have you got?

1 _____

2 _____

7 Read and draw.

1 I've got chicken.

2 I've got ice cream.

8 Draw. Then write.

| cake | fruit | ice cream | juice | pizza |

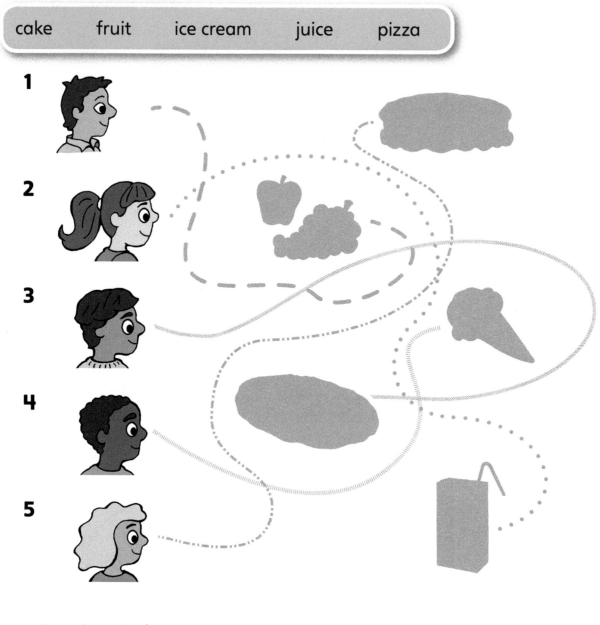

1 What has he got?   He's got _____.

2 What has she got?   She's got _____.

3 What has he got?   He's _____.

4 What has he got?   _____.

5 What has she got?   _____.

9 Look and write.

| biscuits | chips | chocolate | crisps | salt | sugar |

1

_____

2
_____

3
_____

4
_____

5
_____

6
_____

10 Listen, read and circle.

Some foods are salty and some are sweet.
Chocolate is my favourite ¹**salty / sweet** food and
pizza is my favourite ²**salty / sweet** food.

Chips are ³**salty / sweet** and crisps are ⁴**salty /
sweet**, too. They've got ⁵**salt / sugar** on them.

Biscuits, cake and ice cream are all ⁶**salty / sweet**.
They've got ⁷**salt / sugar** in them.

Draw and write.

THINK
BIG

_____
sweet.

_____
salty.

11 **Look and write sweet or salty.**

1  are _____.   2 is _____.

3 are _____.   4 is _____.

5 is _____.   6 are _____.

12 **Find and circle.**

biscuits	cake	chips	chocolate
crisps	ice cream	salty	sweet

p	i	t	e	k	o	c	h	i	p	s
c	h	o	c	o	l	a	t	e	o	a
h	b	i	c	p	o	k	a	w	s	l
o	i	c	e	c	r	e	a	m	w	t
b	i	b	i	s	c	u	i	t	s	y
f	r	d	n	c	c	r	i	s	p	s
r	e	n	f	r	s	w	e	e	t	y

13 **Look, read and** ✓.

1

a He doesn't drink juice. ☐

b He don't drink juice. ☐

2

a She don't eat cake. ☐

b She doesn't eat cake. ☐

3

a They doesn't ride their bikes. ☐

b They don't ride their bikes. ☐

4

a We don't play football. ☐

b We doesn't play football. ☐

14 **Write don't or doesn't and match.**

1 I _____ eat   **a** to work.

2 She _____ go   **b** TV.

3 It _____ drink   **c** pasta.

4 They _____ watch   **d** milk.

15 **Look and circle.**

1 sweets / cake   **2** ice cream / soup   **3** pizza / pie

198
16 **Listen, read and match.**

 **1** I'm Minjoon. It's my birthday! I have seaweed soup. It's salty! I'm from...   **a** Russia.

 **2** My name's Lily. I have a big cake on my birthday. It's very sweet! I'm from...   **b** Mexico.

 **3** I'm Dimitri. On my birthday, I have fruit pie. It's got sugar in it. Mmm! I'm from...   **c** South Korea.

 **4** My name's Anita. I have sweets in a piñata on my birthday. Piñatas are from...   **d** the United States of America.

17 **Look at 16. Complete the table.**

1 _____	the United States	cake
Minjoon	South Korea	2 _____
3 _____	Russia	pie
Anita	4 _____	sweets

18 **Read and find. Write the words.**

ACROSS

4 a favourite day

5 ____ in a piñata

DOWN

1 ____ are from Mexico.

2 a fruit ____

3 a sweet food

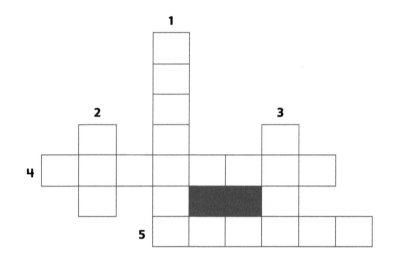

THINK BIG **What do people have on their birthday in your country? Draw.**

19 **Look and write.**

breakfast   dinner   lunch

1 I eat _____ every day.

2 I eat _____ every day.

3 I eat _____ every day.

20 **Draw.**

This is my dinner. I'm eating _____ and _____. I'm drinking _____.

21 **Find and circle the letters l, ll, v and w.**

22 **Read and circle the letters l, ll, v and w.**

1 van **2** leg **3** web **4** doll

23 **Match the words with the same sounds.**

1 let   **a** sell
2 bell   **b** leg
3 vet   **c** win
4 we   **d** van

24 **Listen and chant.**
204

Let's ring the bell
For the vet
With the van!

206 25 🎧 Listen and match. Then write.

1 I've got _____.

2 I've got _____.

water

salad

chicken

chips

pasta

3 I've got _____.

4 I've got _____.

5 I've got _____.

26 Look and write.

1 What has he got?

_____

_____

2 What has she got?

_____

_____

Write I've got, He's got or She's got.

1 What have you got?

_____

milk.

2 What has he got?

_____

pizza.

3 What has she got?

_____

juice.

28 **Colour. Then match and read.**

1 I've got

a fruit.

2 Mum's got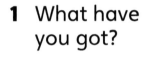

b cake.

3 Dad's got

c ice cream.

29 **Read and circle.**

1 We **don't / doesn't** have a cake on our birthday.

2 Sally **do / doesn't** have soup for breakfast.

3 You **don't / doesn't** sing in the class.

4 The dog **do / doesn't** eat sweets.

Fun and Games

210

1 **Listen and number.**

a   b   c

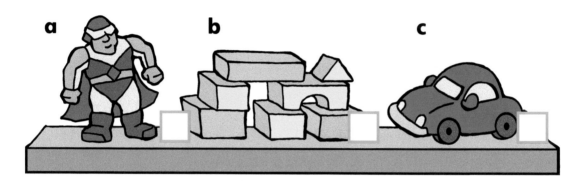

d   e   f

2 **Look at 1 and write.**

| action figure   ball   blocks   car   puppet   train |

1 This is my _____.

2 This is my _____.

3 These are my _____.

4 This is my _____.

5 This is my _____.

6 This is my _____.

3 🎧 **Listen and circle. Then sing.**

214

What's In Your Toy Box?

Kim, what's in your toy box?
Have you got a plane / bike?
No, but this is my blue car / game.
And where's my grey train?

Kim, what's on your toy shelf?
Have you got a ball / doll?
Yes, yes, here it is.
And here's my purple doll / car.

Kim, what's on your table?
Have you got big blocks / stuffed animals?
Yes, and these are my puppets / trains.
My favourite's Mr Fox!

These are my favourite toys,
Purple, green and grey.
I share my toys with my friends
And I play every day!

4 **Draw toys.**

5 **Read and write.**

Where Are My Toys?

Dad, where's my doll?

It's under the table, Jane.

Oh, and where are my action figures?

Here they are. They're on the sofa.

1 Where's the doll?

_____

2 Where are the action figures?

_____

Look. Circle three differences.

THINK BIG

I'm playing with my friends!

I'm playing with my dolls!

6 Read and number.

a

1 It's under the desk. ☐

b

2 They're on the shelf. ☐

c

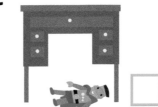

3 It's in the toy box. ☐

7 Write in, on or under.

1 _____

2 _____

3 _____

4 _____

5 _____

6 _____

8 Circle the words and write.

1 x x x i n x x x x x x x   _____

2 x x x x x u n d e r x x   _____

3 x x i n x x x x o n x x   _____

9 Trace and draw.

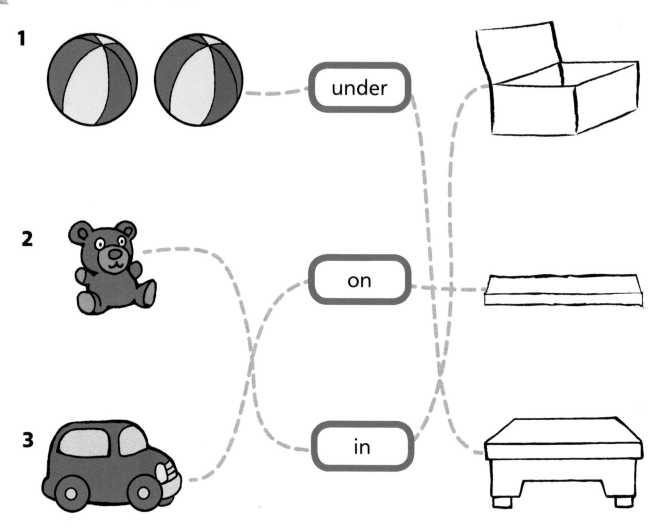

1

2

3

under

on

in

10 Look at 9 and circle.

1 Where are the balls?
The balls are **in** / **on** / **under** the table.

2 Where is the stuffed animal?
The stuffed animal is **in** / **on** / **under** the toy box.

3 Where is the car?
The car is **in** / **on** / **under** the shelf.

11 **Look and match.**

1 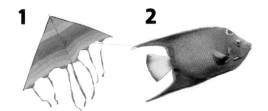 **2** **3** **4** **5**

a dragon   **b** butterfly   **c** kite   **d** fish   **e** bird

12 **Listen and read. Then match and colour.**

220

a 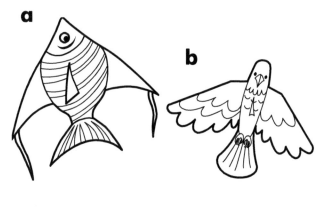   **b**    **c**   **d**

1 This kite looks like a butterfly. It's flying high in the sky. It's big and purple.

2 This kite looks like a bird. It's yellow and brown. This is my favourite kite!

3 This kite looks like a dragon. It's long and very colourful. It's red, orange and green.

4 This is my kite. It looks like a fish. It's blue and red.

13 **Look at 12. Read and circle T for true and F for false.**

1 The purple kite looks like a dragon.   T   F

2 The blue and red kite looks like a fish.   T   F

3 The colourful kite looks like a butterfly.   T   F

4 The yellow and brown kite looks like a bird.   T   F

14 **Find and write the words.**

1 _____   rgnoda

2 _____   drib

3 _____   yflubrett

4 _____   hifs

Guess. Then join the dots and write.

THINK
BIG

1 This kite looks like a _____.

2 This kite looks like a _____.

15 **Look and write There is or There are.**

1 _____ a game.

2 _____ four cars.

3 _____ a puppet.

4 _____ two balls.

16 **Look at 15. Read and circle.**

1 Is there a game?   **Yes, there is. / No, there isn't.**

2 Are there five cars?   **Yes, there are. / No, there aren't.**

3 Is there a stuffed animal?   **Yes, there is. / No, there isn't.**

4 Are there two balls?   **Yes, there are. / No, there aren't.**

17 **Read and write Is there or Are there.**

1 _____ an action figure on the shelf?

2 _____ twelve kites in the sky?

3 _____ dolls in the toy box?

4 _____ a sandwich on the table?

18 **Look and circle.**

1 This train is **woolly / wooden**.

2 These are **Russian / woolly** dolls.

3 These cars are **colourful / wooden**.

19 **Listen, read and match.**

223

1
> This is my toy box. It's got my toys in it. Let's look at them.

a

2
> This is my favourite doll. It's from the U.K. It's a girl. She's wearing a woolly hat and a pink dress.

b

3
> These blocks are very old. They're Dad's blocks. They're wooden. They're from Australia. There are red, blue, green and yellow blocks.

c

20 **Look at 19. Read and match.**

1 There are toys

2 The doll is

3 The blocks come from

4 They're

a her favourite.

b very old.

c in the toy box.

d Australia.

21 **Read and write.**

| colourful | favourite | Russian | wooden | woolly |

1 My _____ toy is my kite.

2 This stuffed animal is wearing a _____ jacket.

3 His bike is red, blue and green. It's very _____.

4 Her action figure is old. It's _____.

5 These dolls are not from the U.K. They're _____.

THINK BIG

What's your favourite toy? Draw and write.

My favourite toy is

_____.

22 **Match.**

a    b    c

1
OK. Thank
you!

2
Sharing is
fun!

3
Here's my car.
Let's share.

23 **Draw.**

I share my toys
with _____.

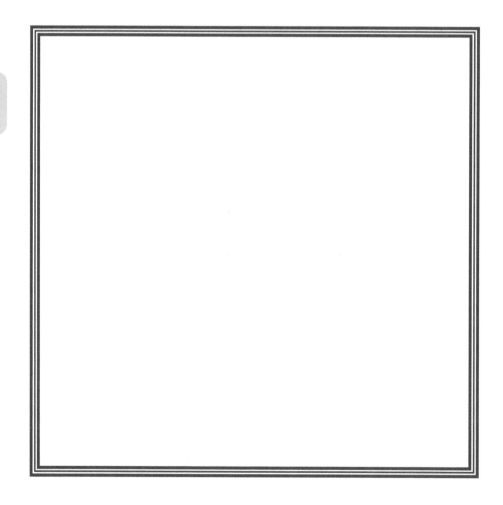

24 **Find and circle the letters qu, x and y.**

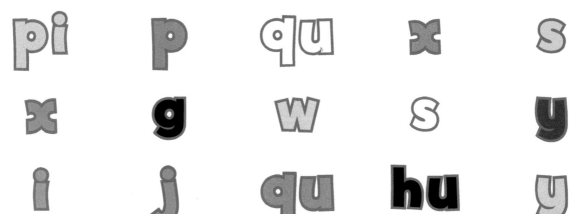

pi p qu x s

x g w s y

i j qu hu y

25 **Read and circle the letters qu, x and y.**

1 (six)   **2** (quick)   **3** (yell)   **4** (box)

26 **Match the words with the same sounds.**

1 quick   **a** yes
2 fox   **b** box
3 yum   **c** quack

27 **Listen and chant.** 229

Six quick foxes,
In a yellow box!

Review

28 **Look and match. Then read.**

John's toys

1   **a** action figure

2   **b** ball

3   **c** blocks

4   **d** plane

5   **e** bike

Jane's toys

6   **f** stuffed animal

7   **g** train

8   **h** doll

9   **i** puppet

10      **j** game

29 **Read and draw.**

Where are the cars?
They're in the toy box.

Where's the ball?
It's on the cars.

231

30 Listen and number.

31 Read and circle. Then look at 30 and ✓ or ✗.

1 **There is / There are** a plane on the shelf. ☐

2 **There is / There are** three action figures under the chair. ☐

3 **There is / There are** a blue ball in the toy box. ☐

4 **There is / There are** two stuffed animals on the chair. ☐

32 Look at 30. Count and write.

How many toys can you see? _____

unit 9 Play Time

1 **Follow the path. Write.**

catching dancing hitting kicking riding
running singing skating skipping throwing

1 _____

2 _____

3 _____

7 _____

6 _____

5 _____

4 _____

8 _____

9 _____

10 _____

2 Listen and sing. Then match.

Play Time Is Cool!

We like play time at our school.
Skipping and dancing,
Throwing and catching.
Play time is cool at our school!

I'm throwing the ball.
It's so much fun!
Are you hitting and running?
Yes, and it's fun.

We're kicking the ball
And trying to score.
It's so much fun.
Let's play some more.

Chorus

1

2

3

4

3 Look at 2 and write.

1 She is _____ the ball.   **2** He is _____ the ball.

3 He is _____.   **4** She is _____ the ball.

4 What are you doing? Draw and write.

I'm _____

_____

5 **Read. Then write.**

1 What's Patrick doing in picture 1?

He's _____.

2 What are the boys doing in picture 2?

They're _____.

3 What are the boys doing in picture 3?

They're _____.

THINK BIG

What do you do before bed?

Look at me. I'm _____.

6 **Look and ✓.**

Is Tom skating?

☐ Yes, he is.
☐ No, he isn't.

Is Jen skipping?

☐ Yes, she is.
☐ No, she isn't.

7 **Look and write the answer.**

Yes, they are.
No, they aren't.

1

Are they playing?

_____

2

Are they jumping?

_____

8 Look, listen and circle.

1

Yes, he is. /
No, he isn't.

2

Yes, she is. /
No, she isn't.

3

Yes, they are. /
No, they aren't.

4

Yes, they are. /
No, they aren't.

9 Look and write.

1

2

Are they playing?
Yes, _____.

Are they kicking a ball?
No, _____.
They're skipping.

10 Look and match.

1 hide and seek

2 climbing

3 tag

4 skipping

5 hopscotch

a

c

b

e

d

11 Listen, read and write.

246

| climbing | hide and seek | hopscotch | skip | tag |

1 Katie and Simon are playing _____. I'm playing, too. It's our favourite game. Hop! Hop! Hop!

2 Emily is _____ the tree. Up! Up! She's at the top! It's very high.

3 The boys are playing _____ in the school playground. George is looking for his friends. Where are they?

4 Tom and Dan are playing _____ with my brother. Run, Dan! Run! Tag, you're it, Tom!

5 My sisters _____ in the playground. It's lots of fun. Jump! Jump! Jump!

12 **Look at 11. Read and ✓ or ✗.**

1 Simon's favourite game is hopscotch. ☐

2 Emily's skipping in the playground. ☐

3 George is at the top of the tree. ☐

4 My brother's playing tag. ☐

5 My sisters are playing hide and seek. ☐

13 **Find and write the words.**

b i m l c n g i

n g i k p i s p

1 _____

2 _____

e h i d n d a e k e s

p h o c h t c o s

a g t

3 _____

4 _____

5 _____

What game do you play? Write.

I _____.

14 **Look and circle.**

1 I **like** / **don't like** fruit.

3 He **likes** / **doesn't like** frogs.

2 She **likes** / **doesn't like** dancing.

4 I **like** / **don't like** salad.

15 **Read and write.**

doesn't	don't	like	likes

1 She _____ like snakes.

2 I don't _____ playing tag.

3 He _____ apples.

4 I _____ like singing.

16 **Draw and write.**

1 I like _____.

2 I don't like _____.

17 **Look and circle.**

1 paper / rock   **2 scissors / rock**   **3 paper / scissors**

18 **Listen, read and match.**

251

1 I'm _____. I'm eight and I'm from Chile. I play a game called Cachipún. My brother is the best player.

a

Michio

2 I'm _____ and I'm nine. I'm from Canada. I play Rock, Paper, Scissors with my sisters and my best friend. I always win.

b

Raúl

3 I'm _____ from Japan. I'm seven. I play this game called Janken at lunch with my friends. I sometimes win.

c

Eva

19 **Look at 18. Read and write the country.**

Canada   Chile   Japan

1 Janken   _____

2 Rock, Paper, Scissors   _____

3 Cachipún   _____

20 **Read and draw.**

1 Paper covers rock.
Paper wins!

2 Scissors cut paper.
Scissors win!

3 Rock breaks scissors.
Rock wins!

THINK BIG **What other game do you play with your hands? Draw.**

_____

21 Match and write.

drink   enough   food   sleep

1

a Get enough _____ and
_____.

2

b Get _____ exercise.

3

c Get enough _____.

22 Draw.

I look after
my body.

23 **Find and circle the letters ss, z and zz.**

24 **Read and circle the letters ss, z and zz.**

1 fizz   **2** mess   **3** zap   **4** miss

25 **Match the words with the same sounds.**

1 zip   **a** zap
2 buzz   **b** hiss
3 miss   **c** fizz

26 **Listen and chant.**

Buzz goes the bee.
Zip, zap!
It misses me!

27 **Look, read and number.**

1 He's catching a ball.   **2** He's throwing a ball.

3 She's kicking a ball.   **4** He's skipping.

5 He likes singing.   **6** She likes dancing.

28 **Draw an activity. Then write.**

I'm _____.

261

29 Listen and number.

30 Read and ✓ or ✗ for you.

1 I get enough exercise.

2 I like hide and seek.

3 I play hopscotch.

4 I get enough sleep.

5 I get enough food and drink.

6 I like tag.

THINK BIG

1 **Look, find and number.** 🔍

2 **Look and ✓.**
What has he got?

My Party List

☐ cars
☐ a bike
☐ a game
☐ a puppet
☐ a train

🔍 **TOYS**

1 action figure
2 bike
3 game
4 puppet

3 **Think and draw.**
What is in the present?

5 cake	**8** catching
6 fruit	**9** kicking
7 juice	**10** throwing

| What **is** it? | It**'s** a chair. |

1 Write and colour.

1 What is it?  ____ a marker pen. It's blue.

2 What _____ it?  ____ a ruler. It's yellow.

3 _____ is it?  ____ a backpack. It's red.

4 What is _____ ?  ____ a crayon. It's green.

5 _____ _____ it?  ____ a pencil. It's blue.

6 What _____ _____ ?  ____ a book. It's red.

2 Join numbers 1 to 10. Look and circle.

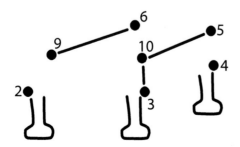

What is it?

It's a **chair** / **desk**.

How many brothers and sisters **have** you **got**? **I've got** one brother.
I've got two sisters.

1 **Write and match.**

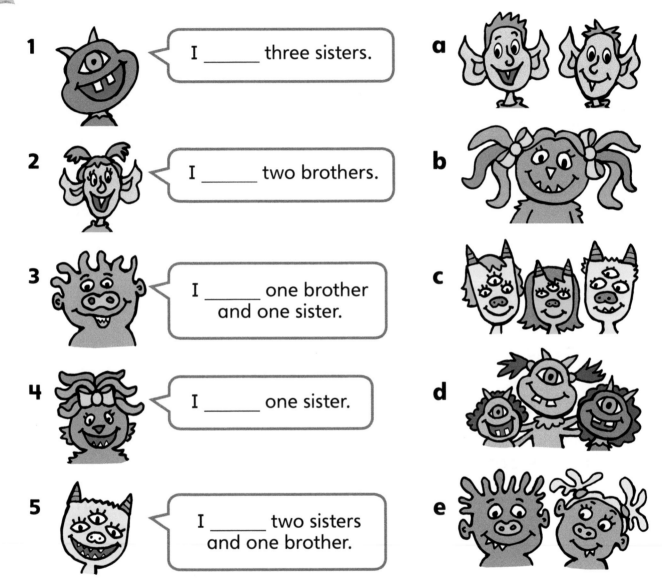

1 I _____ three sisters. a

2 I _____ two brothers. b

3 I _____ one brother and one sister. c

4 I _____ one sister. d

5 I _____ two sisters and one brother. e

2 **Draw a monster family.**

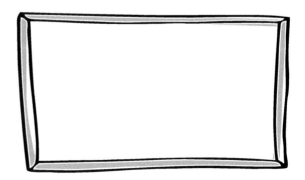

3 **Look at 2.**
Count and write.

How many monsters? _____

Has she **got** long hair?	Yes, she **has**.
Has he **got** short hair?	No, he **hasn't**.
Has it **got** a small head?	Yes, it **has**.
Has it **got** a big head?	No, it **hasn't**.

1 **Look and match.**

1 Has she got a long nose?

2 Has she got short hair?

3 Has she got long arms?

4 Has she got big feet?

Yes, she has.

No, she hasn't.

5 Has he got a long nose?

6 Has he got short hair?

Yes, he has.

7 Has he got long arms?

No, he hasn't.

8 Has he got big feet?

2 **Look at the dog. Write.**

1 It's got long _____.

2 It's got a big _____.

| What **are** you **wearing**? | I**'m wearing** a green hat. |
| What**'s** he/she **wearing**? | He**'s**/She**'s wearing** white trousers. |

1 **What's she wearing? Write and colour.**

1 _____ a red blouse.

2 _____ a yellow skirt.

3 _____ brown shoes.

2 **Read and colour.**

What are you wearing?

I'm wearing a red jacket and brown trousers.

I'm wearing an orange dress and purple shoes.

> What **are** you **doing**?   **I'm** reading.
>
> What**'s** she **doing**?   **She's** making lunch.

1 **Look and write.**

1 What are you doing, Jim?

_____ water.

2 What are you doing, Ellen?

_____ a book.

3 What are you doing, Ben?

_____ my teeth.

4 What are you doing, Pam?

_____ to my dad.

2 **Look at 1. Write.**

1 What's Jim doing? He's _____.

2 What's Ellen doing? _____ reading.

3 What's Ben _____? _____

4 What's Dad _____? _____ watching TV.

What**'s** the duck **doing**?	It**'s swimming**.
What **are** the cows **doing**?	They**'re eating**.
What**'s** he/she **doing**?	He**'s**/She**'s running**.

1 **Look and match. What are they doing?**

1

a sleeping

2

b running

3

c swimming

4

d eating

2 **Read. Circle and write.**

1 What's he doing?    **He's / They're** _____ .

2 What are the cats doing? 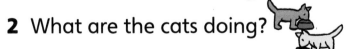   **She's / They're** _____ .

3 What's she doing?    **She's / He's** _____ .

4 What's it doing?   **It's / They're** _____ .

What **has** he **got?**	He**'s got** milk.
What **have** you **got?**	I**'ve got** juice.

1 **Look and write.**

1 What has he got?   He's got **cake** / **milk**.

2 What has she got?   She's got **fruit** / **pasta**.

3 What have you got?   I've got **pizza** / **chocolate**.

4 What have they got?   They've got **crisps** / **juice**.

2 **Write 's got or 've got. Then match.**

1 I _____ juice.   **a**

2 She _____ chicken.   **b**

3 They _____ chips.   **c**

4 He _____ ice cream.   **d**

| **Where**'s the ball? | It's **in** the toy box.
It's **on** the shelf.
It's **under** the table. |
| **Where** are the cars? | They're **under** the desk.
They're **on** the sofa. |

1 **Write Where's or Where are. Then match.**

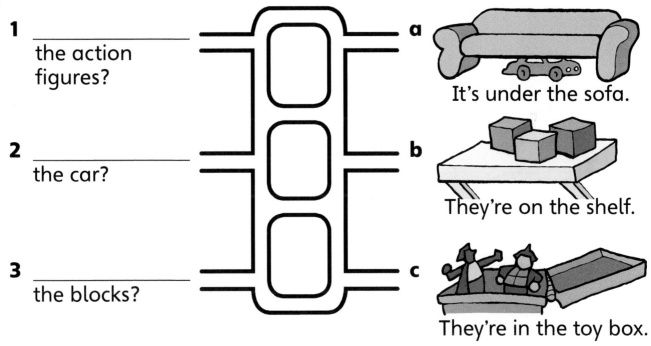

1 _____ the action figures?

2 _____ the car?

3 _____ the blocks?

a It's under the sofa.

b They're on the shelf.

c They're in the toy box.

2 **Look and write in, on or under.**

1 Where's the ball?

It's _____ the desk.

2 Where are the balls?

They're _____ the desk.

3 Where's the ball?

It's _____ the desk.

Is she **singing**?	Yes, she **is**.	No, she **isn't**.
Are they **dancing**?	Yes, they **are**.	No, they **aren't**.

1 Read. Look and write.

1

Is she throwing the ball?

Yes, she _____.

2

Is he running?

No, he _____.

3

Are they sleeping?

No, they _____.

4

Are they skipping?

Yes, they _____.

2 Look at 1. Write Is or Are. Then answer.

1 _____ she eating?

_____

2 _____ he reading?

_____

3 _____ they climbing?

_____

4 _____ they running?

_____

My BIG ENGLISH World

1

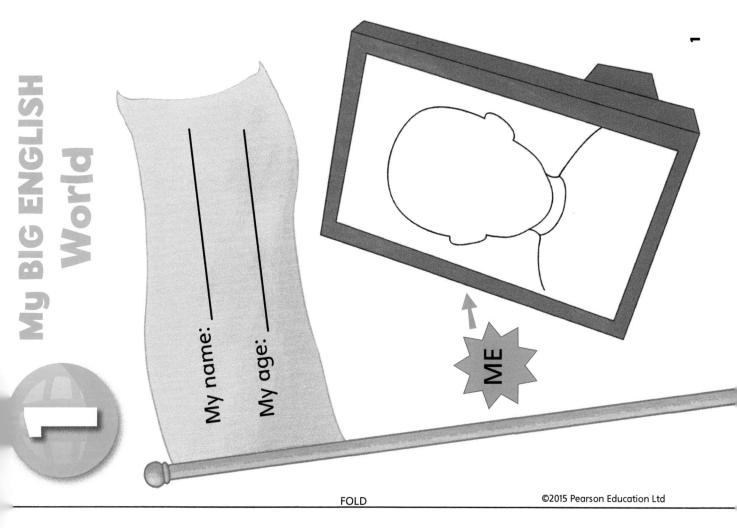

My name: _____

My age: _____

ME →

ENGLISH
AROUND ME

Paste or draw things with English words.

CINEMA TICKET

2

My Favourite Words:

- stuffed animal
- hello • goodbye • pencil
- skipping • finger
- long • mum • pizza

My Favourite Unit:

1 Good Morning, Class!

2 My Family

3 My Body

4 My Favourite Clothes

5 Busy at Home

6 On the Farm

7 Party Time

8 Fun and Games

9 Play Time

FOLD

How are you?

What's your favourite colour?

My Favourite Project:

3